FOUR-LETTER WORD
QUIZZES

First published in 2002 by Miles Kelly Publishing Ltd,
Bardfield Centre, Great Bardfield, Essex, CM7 4SL

ISBN 1-84236-132-5

2 4 6 8 10 9 7 5 3

Project Manager: Ian Paulyn
Assistant: Lisa Clayden
Design: Clare Sleven

Contact us by email: info@mileskelly.net
Website: www.mileskelly.net

Printed in India

FOUR-LETTER WORD
QUIZZES

by
Christopher Rigby

Miles Kelly
PUBLISHING

About the Author

Born in Blackburn, Lancashire in 1960, Christopher Rigby
has been compiling and presenting pub quizzes for the past
15 years. When he is not adding to his material for quizzes,
Christopher works in the car industry. He is married to
Clare – they have two teenage daughters, Hollie and Ashley
and share their home with two demented dogs called Vespa
and Bailey. A keen Manchester United fan Christopher lists
his heroes as George Best and Homer Simpson.

FOUR-LETTER WORD QUIZZES EXPLAINED

This quiz book comprises 900 questions, each of which requires one four letter word for the answer.
Below are a few examples:

1. What is a young sheep called?   (Lamb)
2. What is the capital of Italy?   (Rome)
3. What is the first name of Mr Cleese of Fawlty Towers fame?   (John)

So read on, enjoy and let's keep it clean!

QUIZ ONE

....

WHAT FOUR-LETTER WORD IS DEFINED AS ...

1. The home of a hare?
2. A unit of electrical power?
3. The forepart of a ship?
4. An open case of pastry or sponge cake?
5. A measure of nine inches originally based on the space from the thumb to the extended little finger?
6. An arched roof?
7. A covering for the shoulders or a point of land running into the sea?
8. Selfish or mathematical average?
9. A floating navigational aid?
10. The atmosphere surrounding a person or an object?

ANSWERS
1. Form 2. Watt 3. Prow 4. Flan 5. Span 6. Dome 7. Cape 8. Mean 9. Buoy 10. Aura

QUIZ TWO

1. Which Greek letter of the alphabet also means 'a tiny amount'?
2. In which sport is the Espirito Santo Trophy contested?
3. If 25 equals silver and 50 equals gold, what does 40 equal?
4. Vulcan is the Roman god of what?
5. What is the nickname of Peterborough FC?
6. From which plant is linen obtained?
7. What word was the opposite of allies during the World Wars?
8. Granny and sheepshank are both types of what?
9. Which palindromic pop group had nine No. 1 hits in the UK?
10. Tambour, kettle and bongo are all types of what?

ANSWERS

1. Iota 2. Golf 3. Ruby 4. Fire 5. The Posh 6. Flax 7. Axis 8. Knot 9. Abba 10. Drum

QUIZ THREE

1. What does a calorimeter measure?
2. What is the name of the backing group of Desmond Decker?
3. Chieftain, Leopard and Sherman are all types of what?
4. What name is given to the period of 40 days before Easter?
5. Which company invented the Walkman?
6. What was designed by Alec Issigonis and launched in 1959?
7. What is a querquedule?
8. In the *Star Wars* films what is the name of the Jedi knight who informed Luke Skywalker that Princess Leia was his sister?
9. What is the Russian equivalent for the name of John?
10. Name the singer who won the Eurovision Song Contest with the song 'All Kinds Of Everything'?

ANSWERS

1. Heat 2. Aces 3. Tank 4. Lent 5. Sony 6. The Mini 7. A duck 8. Yoda 9. Ivan 10. Dana

QUIZ FOUR

1. What is the name of the Roman counterpart of the Greek goddess Hera?

2. Into which sea does the River Jordan empty?

3. What kind of animal represents the star sign of Taurus?

4. To which flower family does garlic belong?

5. What is the name of the main national airport of Paris?

6. What is the collective noun for a group of angels?

7. A hart's tongue is a type of what?

8. The Belmonts were the backing band of which singer who topped the charts with 'The Wanderer'?

9. What does the musical term 'largo' mean?

10. According to the Bible who was the first ever person to get drunk and to see a rainbow?

ANSWERS

1. Juno 2. Dead 3. Bull 4. Lily 5. Orly 6. Host 7. Fern 8. Dion 9. Slow 10. Noah

QUIZ FIVE

1. What name is given to a stream in Scotland?
2. Which English city is the site of 30 houses that are collectively known as the Royal Crescent?
3. Name the island on the west coast of Scotland which is the site of a monastery called St Columba's.
4. Which British industry was nationalised on New Year's Day in 1947?
5. What is nicknamed 'The Garden of England'?
6. What is the name of the airport that serves the city of Aberdeen?
7. What is the name of London's largest park?
8. In which Irish county could a person actually kiss the Blarney Stone?
9. The Great Smoo is Scotland's largest what?
10. Name the two major rivers both with four letters in their name that flow through the city of York.

QUIZ SIX

1. In a TV advert for what could you have heard the publicity slogan 'Watch out, there's a Humphrey about'?

2. What name is given to the vibrating mouthpiece on a musical instrument?

3. If an object is described as campanulate it is shaped like a what?

4. Name the singer who charted with the song 'Kiss From A Rose'.

5. What popular name for a family pet derives from the Latin meaning 'I trust'?

6. What colour is Australia's counterpart for the *Yellow Pages*?

7. What name is given to a cross between a mare and an ass?

8. In America what is the name of the TV award which is equivalent to a film Oscar?

9. Name the island that lies between Italy and Corsica.

10. In gymnastics what is 5 metres long?

ANSWERS

1. Milk 2. Reed 3. Bell 4. Seal 5. Fido 6. Pink 7. Mule 8. Emmy 9. Elba 10. Beam

QUIZ SEVEN

1. If ducks quack and dogs bark, what are donkeys said to do?
2. The product hessian is obtained from which plant?
3. Sausage and mash is cockney rhyming slang for what?
4. Derek Dick was the real name of which singer known by a single four-letter name?
5. What name is given to a two-masted Arab sailing vessel?
6. What nickname was bestowed upon the jazz musician Charlie Parker?
7. Who rode an eight-legged horse called Sleipner?
8. Which company employs the publicity slogan 'Means happy motoring'?
9. What name is given to the unit of measurement used for the weighing of fish?
10. When canvas is coated with oxidised linseed oil what does it become?

ANSWERS
1. Bray 2. Jute 3. Cash 4. Fish 5. Dhow 6. Bird 7. Odin 8. Esso 9. Cran 10. Lino

QUIZ EIGHT

1. What sort of animal is a slang term for £25?
2. If a person has committed a crime known as regicide who or what has he killed?
3. A tandoor is a clay what?
4. What name is given to an image of a saint in art?
5. What is the name of the local pub in the soap opera *Brookside*?
6. What is an inverted stitch in knitting called?
7. What is the traditional symbol for a fifth wedding anniversary?
8. In which war was the term concentration camp first used?
9. King Priam was the last ruler of which ancient city?
10. What name is given to the symbol at the beginning of a musical stave that indicates the pitch?

QUIZ NINE

1. What name is given to the central part of a church?
2. What type of object would be of particular interest to a bibliophile?
3. In cricket what name is given to the fielding position closest to behind the wicket?
4. What common word is a shortened version of the word perambulator?
5. What is the name of the fungal disease that affects oats?
6. What turns litmus paper red?
7. Kodiak, Alaskan, black and brown are all species of what?
8. What is the English equivalent of an American streetcar?
9. What kind of fish is traditionally eaten by Polish people on Christmas Day?
10. Name the German pop act who first charted in 1997 with the song 'Encore Une Fois'.

QUIZ TEN

1. Which drink, one of Shakespeare's favourite tipples, is distilled from honey?
2. A prune is a dried what?
3. What is the name of the vegetable which is also known as lady's fingers?
4. What is the field of expertise of an oenophile?
5. Blue fin and skipjack are both types of what?
6. With regard to champagne which four-letter word means very dry?
7. From which animal is feta cheese obtained?
8. What sort of foodstuff is measured in coombs?
9. In Mexico what name is given to a fried stuffed pancake?
10. When milk curdles what name is given to the liquid that runs from the curd?

ANSWERS
1. Mead 2. Plum 3. Okra 4. Wine 5. Tuna 6. Brut 7. Goat 8. Corn 9. Taco 10. Whey

QUIZ ONE

....

WHAT FOUR-LETTER WORD IS DEFINED AS ...

1. A raised platform at the end of a hall?
2. A dumb person?
3. A joke meant to deceive people?
4. A bluish white precious stone?
5. The rod on which a wheel turns?
6. The Russian word for emperor?
7. The chief clergyman in a cathedral church?
8. The ashes of seaweed used for making iodine?
9. The sand left when water flows away?
10. The spear or hook used by fishermen for landing fish?

QUIZ TWO

1. What name is given to an area which is equivalent to one quarter of an acre?
2. What is the name of the Hawaiian dish that consists of steamed meat and plant leaves?
3. What sort of creature would provide the staple diet of a vermivorous animal?
4. What name is given to a thin metal strip on the neck of a guitar?
5. In which city is the Taj Mahal?
6. What was the favoured item of attire for citizens of ancient Rome?
7. Gene Simmons and Ace Frehley are both members of which rock band?
8. By what name is French Sudan now known?
9. Who is the Patron Saint of Lost Causes?
10. Which German group had their only UK hit in 1982 with a song called 'Da Da Da'?

ANSWERS
1. Rood 2. Luau 3. A worm 4. Fret 5. Agra 6. Toga 7. Kiss 8. Mali 9. Jude 10. Trio

QUIZ THREE

1. Which popular children's toy was invented by Ole and Godtfred Christiansen?
2. Where on a ship would you find the lubber's hole?
3. What is the more common name for the tam tam, a percussion instrument that originated in China?
4. In falconry what name is given to the leather strap that is attached to the leg of the bird?
5. What is the female equivalent to a knight?
6. What was the surname of the man of the cloth who won the Nobel Peace Prize in 1984?
7. What do Americans call the bonnet of a car?
8. Portree is the main town on which island?
9. In brewing what is a spile?
10. In which Carla Lane-penned TV programme did Felicity Kendal play a character called Gemma Palmer?

QUIZ FOUR

1. What name is given to an inner tower of a castle?
2. What is the horn of a rhinoceros made from?
3. What sort of meat is used in the preparation of wiener schnitzel?
4. Van Morrison fronted which pop group in the 1960s who had a hit with the song 'Here Comes The Night'?
5. In which mountain range is the Matterhorn?
6. Which inert gas is used to illuminate advertising signs?
7. For which 1981 film did Warren Beatty receive a Best Director Oscar?
8. What was last seen alive on the island of Mauritius in 1681?
9. Which South American city shares its name with a type of bean?
10. What sort of bird is considered to be sacred in Egypt?

ANSWERS

1. Keep 2. Hair 3. Veal 4. Them 5. Alps 6. Neon 7. Reds 8. Dodo 9. Lima 10. Ibis

QUIZ FIVE

**WHAT FOUR-LETTER WORD CAN FOLLOW EACH
GROUP OF THREE WORDS?
E.G. CLOCK, BABY, CLIFF = FACE,
I.E. CLOCK FACE, BABY FACE, CLIFF FACE.**

1. French, fog, shoe.
2. Mud, bird, bed.
3. Bottle, river, blood.
4. Battle, court, star.
5. Base, beach, eye.
6. Turn, over, rain.
7. Oil, table, head.
8. Gold, flat, cat.
9. Wet, dinner, space.
10. Clock, green, credit.

QUIZ SIX

1. What was the name of the sailing vessel in which Jason sailed in search of the Golden Fleece?
2. England's highest waterfall is called the Cauldron Snout. On which river does it stand?
3. What is the official language of Pakistan?
4. In the Oxford and Cambridge boat race what is the name of the Oxford reserve crew?
5. How many points is gold worth in archery?
6. Which famous American university is located at New Haven in Connecticut?
7. In which country could you spend kips in the city of Vientiane?
8. What do Americans call a waistcoat?
9. What is a meerschaum?
10. What was the name of the bad-mannered puppet pooch who partnered Bob Carolgees?

ANSWERS
1. Argo 2. Tees 3. Urdu 4. Isis 5. Nine 6. Yale 7. Laos 8. Vest 9. A pipe 10. Spit

QUIZ SEVEN

1. In the sport of yachting what name is given to the sailing manoeuvre whereby you change direction to face an oncoming wind?
2. On which island is the Indonesian capital of Jakarta?
3. In athletics which city hosts the Bislett Games?
4. What is the name of the Hindu goddess of destruction?
5. On which river is the Aswan Dam?
6. In mythology a silkie is half man, and half what?
7. Which sport was included in the Summer Olympics for the first time in 1964, because it was specially requested by the host nation?
8. What name is given to the grated rind of a lemon?
9. In which town did Jesus perform his first miracle when he turned water into wine?
10. Which model of Renault car shares its name with the Greek muse of history?

ANSWERS
1. Luff 2. Java 3. Oslo 4. Kali 5. Nile 6. Seal 7. Judo 8. Zest 9. Cana 10. Clio

QUIZ EIGHT

....

1. What did Paul Newman eat 50 of to win a bet in the film *Cool Hand Luke*?
2. In nuclear reactors what sort of metal acts as a shield?
3. What name is given to a male salmon?
4. Which American wrestler plays the role of the Scorpion King in the 2001 film sequel to *The Mummy*?
5. Which English river would you associate with the nickname of William Shakespeare?
6. Which 1995 film directed by Michael Mann co-starred Al Pacino, Robert de Niro, Val Kilmer and Jon Voight?
7. What word can mean both a vertical wall of water and a monotonous person?
8. Who topped the UK singles charts in 1984 with the song '99 Red Balloons'?
9. Which film company opened its films with Bombadier Wells striking a large gong?
10. What name is given to the member of a film crew who moves the film equipment?

QUIZ NINE

1. Who is the Norse God of thunder?
2. In which film did Jack Nicholson play the lycanthrope lover of Michelle Pfeiffer?
3. In *Treasure Island* what was Long John Silver's job aboard the *Hispaniola*?
4. Rat, toad and badger. What creature is missing from this literary quartet?
5. What was the title of the 1984 mini series starring Phoebe Cates, based on a novel by Shirley Conran?
6. What is the name of the aniseed-based drink that is extremely popular in Greece?
7. What was the title of the best-selling Human League album that featured their No. 1 hit 'Don't You Want Me'?
8. In mythology what is the name of the River of Hate, that flows through the underworld?
9. On which island is the town of Tobermory?
10. What sort of bird returned to Noah's ark with a branch in its beak?

QUIZ TEN

....

NAME THE FOUR-LETTER WORD NO. I HITS THAT THE FOLLOWING ARTISTS RECORDED IN THE GIVEN YEARS.

1. 1965 – The Beatles
2. 1992 – Shakespeare's Sister
3. 1979 – The Village People
4. 1979 – Gary Numan
5. 1958 – The Kalin Twins
6. 1980 – Dexy's Midnight Runners
7. 1983 – Spandau Ballet
8. 1982 – Irene Cara
9. 1968 – The Crazy World of Arthur Brown
10. 1977 – Deniece Williams

QUIZ ONE

....

WHAT FOUR-LETTER SURNAME IS SHARED BY ...

1. Mrs Fatboy Slim, the youngest player in England's 1966 World Cup winning team and the lady who co-founded Desilu Productions?

2. The actor who plays Dave Best in *The Royle Family*, a former tennis Champion and a country singer nicknamed 'The Man in Black'?

3. The actor who won an Oscar for the film *Shine*, the female vocalist who topped the charts with 'Power Of Love' and a former Welsh and Liverpool striker?

4. The Foreign Secretary at the end of the 20th century, the captain of the *Endeavour* and Dudley Moore's partner in *Not Only But Also*?

5. The director of *The Sound Of Music*, the partner of Eric Bartholomew and the footballer who captained the FA Cup winners in 2000?

6. The singers who had hits with 'Bionic Santa', 'Edelweiss' and 'Ernie'

7. The longest serving DJ on Radio One, Diana Rigg's character in *The Avengers* and the man after whom policemen are nicknamed Bobbies?

8. The actor who played Pete Beale, a policeman who became a skating World Champion and the star of the film *Rebel Without A Cause*?

9. The actor who played Flash Harry in the St Trinian's films, the singer who had a hit with 'Pink Cadillac' and a nursery-rhyme character who was a merry old soul?

10. The actor eaten by a shark on film, the author of *Pygmalion* and the first British winner of the Eurovision Song Contest?

ANSWERS

1. BALL – Zoe, Alan, Lucille 2. CASH – Craig, Pat, Johnny 3. RUSH – Geoffrey, Jennifer, Ian 4. COOK – Robin, James, Peter 5. WISE – Robert, Ernie, Dennis 6. HILL – Chris, Vince, Benny 7. PEEL – John, Emma, Robert 8. DEAN – Peter, Christopher, James 9. COLE – George, Natalie, Old King 10. SHAW – Robert, George Bernard, Sandie

QUIZ TWO

1. What was the name of the dragon who was the best friend of Jackie Paper?
2. Who did George Takei play in *Star Trek*?
3. In the world of nature what has a central vein known as a mid-rib?
4. What is the name of the car driven by Michael Knight in *Knight Rider*?
5. Which brewery uses a red triangle as its trademark?
6. What was the title of the film in which Richard Dreyfuss played a lawyer defending Barbra Streisand in court?
7. Who had a No. 1 hit with 'Orinoco Flow'?
8. The sousaphone is the largest member of which family of instruments?
9. Vitu Levu is the largest island in which island group?
10. The word sabotage derived from an item of footwear called a sabot. What is a sabot?

ANSWERS
1. Puff 2. Sulu 3. Leaf 4. Kitt 5. Bass 6. Nuts 7. Enya 8. Tuba 9. Fiji 10. Clog

QUIZ THREE

1. What is the name of the eldest Tracy brother in *Thunderbirds*?
2. What is the name of the river that flows through the city of Lancaster?
3. Elephant, fur and crabeater are all species of which animal?
4. Laverock was an old-fashioned name for which bird?
5. Which spice is obtained from the outer shell of a nutmeg?
6. Nanny goat is Cockney rhyming slang for what in the world of horse-racing?
7. What name is given by photographers, to the lotion in which they develop their films?
8. Where in the human body are the metatarsal arches located?
9. In which card game is a prial of threes the top hand?
10. In the world of physics what does a capital letter V indicate?

QUIZ FOUR

1. Name the pop group fronted by Midge Ure in the 1970s that topped the charts with a song called 'Forever And Ever'.
2. What name is given to the family groups that dolphins travel in?
3. What kind of meat is used to make pastrami?
4. What is the highest volcano in Europe?
5. Which animated film featured the voices of Sharon Stone, Sylvester Stallone and Gene Hackman?
6. What is the name of the canal that connects the Baltic Sea to the North Sea?
7. Which first name for a boy is also the Italian word for eight?
8. What name is given to the highest point of a triangle?
9. Ash Wednesday is the first day of what?
10. What sort of marine creature is a quahog, some of which can live for up to 200 years?

ANSWERS
1. Slik 2. Pods 3. Beef 4. Etna 5. Antz 6. Kiel 7. Otto 8. Apex 9. Lent 10. Clam

QUIZ FIVE

**WHAT FOUR-LETTER WORD CAN PRECEDE EACH
GROUP OF THREE WORDS?
E.G. SITE, FIRE, BED = CAMP,
I.E. CAMP SITE, CAMP FIRE, CAMP BED.**

1. Stone, light, walk
2. House, yard, hand
3. Saddle, street, board
4. Worm, measure, deck
5. Man, bell, step
6. Teeth, shake, bottle
7. Ball, lights, note
8. Sock, break, mill
9. Age, man, code
10. Drill, engine, exit

QUIZ SIX

1. Which bird indigenous to South America is related to the ostrich?
2. What was the name of the lioness in *Born Free*?
3. What have you purchased if you have taken out a mortgage known as bottomry?
4. Which part of the foot is also the name of a fish?
5. Pulex irritans is the scientific name for a what?
6. What sort of attire is a filibeg?
7. What is the alternative name for a cougar or mountain lion?
8. What is the national flower of England?
9. What is the name of the second largest city in Poland?
10. In weaving what name is given to the thread in a shuttle?

ANSWERS
1. Rhea 2. Elsa 3. Boat or ship 4. Sole 5. Flea 6. Kilt 7. Puma 8. Rose 9. Lodz 10. Weft

QUIZ SEVEN

1. In a court of law what name is given to the area where the accused sits?
2. In Greek mythology who visited his lover Leda in the guise of a swan?
3. What is a linden tree also known as?
4. What is the weakest piece in a game of chess?
5. What kind of drink can be vintage and ruby?
6. In which country is the source of the River Amazon?
7. Which American sitcom featured the antics of the Sunshine Cab Company?
8. What is measured by a pluviometer?
9. Which dessert is obtained from the starch in a palm tree?
10. What was the name of the scarecrow in *The Wizard of Oz*?

QUIZ EIGHT

1. Which gambling implements are nicknamed 'Devil's bones'?
2. Which famous London statue was sculpted by Sir Alfred Gilbert?
3. What is the name of the island that lies off the north coast of Malta?
4. By what four-letter name is the pop star Robert Bell known when backed by his gang?
5. Which dynasty was founded in 1368 by a gentleman called Chu Yuan Chang?
6. What is the name of the fluid secreted by the liver?
7. What type of tree is the most prolific producer of the fossil resin amber?
8. What is the name of the river that flows through the city of Cardiff?
9. Which unit of land measurement is equivalent to 4,840 square yards?
10. What word for a violent criminal is derived from a Hindu sect who murdered and robbed travellers?

QUIZ NINE

1. On which Hawaiian island is Pearl Harbor?
2. What name is given to a solo performance in an opera?
3. What sort of axe used by blacksmiths and coopers has a blade that is set at a right angle to the handle?
4. What animal is depicted on the flag of Tasmania?
5. By what four-letter name is Richard Hall better known in the world of pop music?
6. Frog and toad is Cockney rhyming slang for what?
7. The mangelwurzel is a member of which vegetable family?
8. Who were the first British pop group to tour China?
9. What sort of cat can be described as ecudate?
10. Name the three No. 1's for Take That, each of which have just four letters in the song title?

ANSWERS
1. Oahu 2. Aria 3. Adze 4. Lion 5. Moby 6. Road 7. Beet 8. Wham 9. Manx i.e. no tail 10. 'Babe', 'Pray' and 'Sure'.

QUIZ TEN

1. What is the name of the parliament in Japan?
2. Ndajamena is the capital city of which African country?
3. In which Russian river was Rasputin drowned?
4. Which country was thrown out of the Organisation of American States in 1962?
5. In which country are the Zagros Mountains?
6. What is the capital of South Yemen?
7. On which river does the city of Hamburg stand?
8. Which island's parliament is called the Court of Chief Pleas?
9. Columbus is the state capital of which American state?
10. What is the currency unit of Bangladesh?

QUIZ ONE

....

NAME THE FOUR-LETTER SURNAMES OF THE
FOLLOWING FOOTBALLERS.

1. Who was the youngest footballer to score for England in the 20th century?

2. Who was voted Footballer of the Year in 1968 and European Footballer of the Year the following season?

3. Who scored a headed goal in the 1984 FA Cup final and went on to become a TV football pundit?

4. Who was the youngest player in Sven Goran Eriksson's first England squad?

5. Who scored two goals in the 1958 World Cup Final?

6. Who scored the first ever goal to be featured on BBC's *Match Of The Day* and went on to be a World Cup winner with England?

7. Who left Manchester United to manage Blackburn Rovers and has since been appointed David O'Leary's assistant at Leeds United?

8. Who was the first Italian footballer to be voted Footballer of the Year in England?

9. Who was the first black player to captain England?

10. Who was the first Frenchman to be voted European Footballer of the Year?

QUIZ TWO

1. What is the currency unit in South Africa?
2. Which car company has a badge that consists of four linked circles?
3. What is the highest male singing voice?
4. What is the name of the valley near San Francisco that is an important wine growing area?
5. What name is given to a young whale?
6. What is the alternative name for a castle in chess?
7. What is the name of the hero in the Disney animation *A Bug's Life*?
8. When iron oxidises what is formed?
9. What four-letter word is shouted by sailors in order to gain attention?
10. According to the Bible what musical instrument was played by David?

ANSWERS
1. Rand 2. Audi 3. Alto 4. Napa 5. Calf 6. Rook 7. Flik 8. Rust 9. Ahoy 10. Harp

QUIZ THREE

1. What white wine from Germany shares its name with a joint of ham?
2. Name the African female recording artist who released a million-selling 1980s album called *Diamond Life*.
3. What was the title of the opera that was composed to commemorate the opening of the Suez Canal?
4. In the Disney film *The Lion King* what is the name of Simba's evil uncle?
5. To which plant family does garlic belong?
6. What nautical term is the name given to the left side of a ship?
7. What name is given to the church receptacle that houses the water used in baptisms?
8. What is the name of the heaviest sword used in Olympic fencing competitions?
9. Garden and Little Marvels are both types of which vegetable?
10. Michael Foale was the first British astronaut to do what in space?

ANSWERS
1. Hock 2. Sade 3. *Aida* 4. Scar 5. Lily 6. Port 7. Font 8. Epee 9. Peas 10. Walk

QUIZ FOUR

1. What is the name of Dame Edna Everage's husband?
2. Which singing voice comes directly below a baritone?
3. What is the traditional gift given on the seventh wedding anniversary?
4. What is the name of the backing band of Desmond Dekker?
5. Avarice, envy, gluttony, pride, sloth, wrath. What is missing?
6. On which river does the city of Leeds stand?
7. What name is given to a group of cattle, horses or deer?
8. What is the first name of Miss Marple?
9. By what more common name is clarified pig fat known?
10. What name is give to the young of a zebra?

QUIZ FIVE

1. What was the name of Dick Van Dyke's sweep in *Mary Poppins*?

2. What is the name of TV detective Colombo's pet basset hound?

3. Between 1900 and 1960 what was the most popular papal name?

4. What is the name of Clint Eastwood's son who co-starred with him in the film *Honky Tonk Man*?

5. What is the first name of the classical composer Stravinsky?

6. What is the name of Mick Jagger's gem of a daughter?

7. What is the real first name of Ozzy Osbourne of Black Sabbath fame?

8. In the TV advert what is the name of Homepride's chief flour-grader?

9. Which classic novel featured a building called Donwell Abbey, the home of Mr Knightley?

10. Which first name links the lead female characters in the films *Top Hat* and *Flash Gordon*?

ANSWERS
1. Bert 2. Fang 3. Pius 4. Kyle 5. Igor 6. Jade 7. John 8. Fred 9. *Emma* 10. Dale

QUIZ SIX

1. What is the name of the sea that spans the countries of Kazakhstan and Uzbekistan?
2. Frame and dome are both types of what?
3. What are kept in an apiary?
4. What is the traditional gift given on the fourth wedding anniversary?
5. Which city hosted the 1987 World Athletics Championships?
6. Which boy's name is also a name given to a whirlpool?
7. What title is the British equivalent of a European count?
8. What was the surname of the man responsible for the first mass-produced ball-point pen?
9. What was the title of the song that provided a 1984 Top 10 hit on both sides of the Atlantic for the rock group Van Halen?
10. What was the name of the official Soviet news agency?

ANSWERS
1. Aral 2. Tent 3. Bees 4. Silk 5. Rome 6. Eddy 7. Earl 8. Biro 9. 'Jump' 10. Tass

QUIZ SEVEN

1. What title was given to the chief magistrate in ancient Venice?
2. What is the name of the companion of Scooby Doo, who wears a yellow cravat?
3. Which character was played by Brent Spiner in *Star Trek The Next Generation*?
4. What is the alternative name for a water rat?
5. Which girl's name is also the name of the house in the novel *Gone With The Wind*?
6. What name is given to a group of wolves?
7. What did the R stand for in the name of JR Ewing?
8. What is the fruit of the blackthorn bush called?
9. Who captained the *Pequod* in *Moby-Dick*?
10. There are 16 what in a rupee?

ANSWERS
1. Doge 2. Fred 3. Data 4. Vole 5. Tara 6. Pack 7. Ross 8. Sloe 9. Ahab 10. Anna

QUIZ EIGHT

1. What provides the staple diet of nucivorous creatures?
2. According to the Bible whose was the first birth?
3. What is the medical name for the bone in the forearm next to the radius?
4. Which musical instrument was jazz musician Charlie Mingus famous for playing?
5. There are 20 fluid ounces in a what?
6. Which is the largest country in the world with a four-letter name?
7. Which 1982 song provided the only Top 10 hit for Fat Larry's Band?
8. What is the predicative word in a sentence?
9. Which Fleetwood Mac album shares its name with a long tooth protruding from the mouth?
10. There are four types of weather that are collectively known as precipitation. One is sleet, name the other three.

QUIZ NINE

1. A tarantula hawk is a type of what?
2. What was the name of the hairy twin brother of Jacob in the Bible?
3. Which 2000 hit for Gabrielle sampled the Bob Dylan classic 'Knocking On Heaven's Door'?
4. Which boy's name is also the name given to low ground between hills?
5. What surname connects St Paul's Cathedral and the novel *Beau Geste*?
6. What is the first name of the supermodel who acquired the nickname of 'The Body'?
7. What sort of creatures did the central character of the novel *1984* have a morbid fear of?
8. What is the name of the sweet fruit of the palm tree?
9. Which 1964 film based on a 19th-century historical event co-starred Stanley Baker and Michael Caine?
10. Which boy band covered the Queen song 'We Will Rock You'?

ANSWERS
1. Wasp 2. Esau 3. 'Rise' 4. Dale 5. Wren – the architect Sir Christopher Wren and the author PC Wren 6. Elle 7. Rats 8. Date 9. Zulu 10. Five

QUIZ TEN

1. What does the adjective costal refer to?
2. What would you be losing if you were desquamating?
3. What four-letter adjective would describe an ectomorph body?
4. What is caused by inflammation of the sebaceous glands?
5. If a person is suffering from microcephaly, what part of their body would be abnormally small?
6. What name is given to a shoemaker's model of the human foot?
7. A deficiency of what causes anaemia?
8. What is studied by a trichologist?
9. What is caused by excess uric acid in the blood?
10. What is the proper term for a rabbit's tail?

ANSWERS
1. Ribs 2. Skin 3. Thin 4. Acne 5. Head 6. Last 7. Iron 8. Hair 9. Gout 10. Scut

QUIZ ONE

WHAT FOUR-LETTER WORD IS DEFINED AS ...

1. A solid body having six equal square faces?
2. The service of the Lord's Supper in the Roman Catholic Church?
3. The outer skin of grain?
4. A man-eating giant of fairytales?
5. The foam created by the dashing of waves?
6. A thin cloth worn to hide the face?
7. The fibre obtained from coconuts?
8. An image worshipped as a god?
9. To cut off or clip the horns of an animal?
10. The written part of a book?

ANSWERS
1. Cube 2. Mass 3. Bran 4. Ogre 5. Surf 6. Veil 7. Coir 8. Idol 9. Poll 10. Text

QUIZ TWO

1. What are dried in an oasthouse?
2. In computing 8 bits equal 1 what?
3. In May 2001 in which town did John Prescott punch an egg-wielding protestor?
4. Which snail-like animal with no shell shares its name with a piece of metal used as a bullet?
5. What title was given to a king in Persia?
6. What word links a group of hawks with a list of actors?
7. What is the name of the heavy staff carried by the Speaker of the House of Commons?
8. What soothing balm with three vowels in its name is obtained from the cactus plant?
9. What word links a plant, a toffee and a coin-making establishment?
10. Kaur is the last name taken by all women that adhere to which religion?

QUIZ THREE

1. What is the Scottish word for straits?
2. Reputedly whose last words were 'What an artist the world is losing in me'?
3. Which part of a ship shares its name with a city in Yorkshire?
4. He was born James Bradford. What did he change his surname to when he became an actor?
5. In the US Army what shorter name was given to a general-purpose vehicle?
6. What is the smallest number that is not a prime number?
7. What sport are you not allowed to play left-handed?
8. In the 1930s and 1940s who did Maureen O'Sullivan play in six films?
9. What pen-name did the novelist Hector Hugh Munro adopt?
10. What does the P stand for on a bottle of brandy bearing the initials VSOP?

ANSWERS
1. Kyle 2. Nero 3. Hull 4. Nail – Jimmy Nail 5. Jeep 6. Four 7. Polo 8. Jane – in the *Tarzan films* 9. Saki 10. Pale

QUIZ FOUR

1. Which part of a house could be built in a mansard style?
2. Name the film that featured the songs 'Out Here On My Own' and 'I Sing The Body Electric'.
3. What is a cricket umpire signalling with both his arms outstretched?
4. What four-letter word connects the nicknames of Mike Tyson and Margaret Thatcher?
5. What is the 1989 film starring Ally Sheedy as a psychic who taps into the mind of a serial killer, who also happens to be a psychic?
6. Which saint's day falls on October 18th?
7. Which song was a hit for both Tom Jones and Prince?
8. In EastEnders the character of Ian Beale is the father of twins. His son is called Peter, what is his daughter called?
9. Which member of the Monty Python team has a four-letter first name and a four-letter surname?
10. In which American TV series did Robert Guillaume first play the role of Benson the butler?

ANSWERS
1. Roof 2. Fame 3. Wide 4. Iron 5. Fear 6. Luke 7. 'Kiss' 8. Lucy 9. Eric Idle 10. Soap

QUIZ FIVE

WHAT IS THE SURNAME OF ...

1. The crooner who died in May 2001 aged 88?
2. The doctor who Burke and Hare stole bodies for?
3. Roy of the Rovers?
4. The man who discovered a vaccine for polio?
5. William Broad, who became a punk-rock singer?
6. The man who invented the synthesiser?
7. The singer who topped the charts with the song 'Tears On My Pillow' in 1975?
8. The man who invented the revolver in 1835?
9. The first American woman in space?
10. The first ever teenager to have a UK No. 1 hit single?

QUIZ SIX

1. In the Bible who was known as the Father of the Human Race?
2. The name of which board game is derived from the Latin for 'I play'?
3. There are four main lines in palmistry, one of which is the heart line. Name the other three, each of which have four letters in their name.
4. Berlin became the capital of the reunified Germany. What was the capital of West Germany before the Berlin Wall was dismantled?
5. What type of creature is a natterjack?
6. What is the title of the political party member who enforces discipline?
7. What is the most southerly county on the Emerald Isle?
8. What does a testator make?
9. Aqua Sulis was the Roman name for which English city?
10. What would a person do in a plebiscite?

ANSWERS
1. Adam 2. Ludo 3. Life, head and fate 4. Bonn 5. Toad 6. Whip 7. Cork 8. A will 9. Bath 10. Vote

QUIZ SEVEN

1. Which Ukrainian city gave its name to a chicken dish?
2. A hautboy is what kind of musical instrument?
3. What name is given to an Indian dish of spiced lentils?
4. On which lake does the city of Buffalo stand in America?
5. Gingivitis affects what part of the body?
6. What is the name of the cape located at the southern tip of South America?
7. Which model married David Bowie and went on to star in the film *Star Trek the Undiscovered Country* in which she played a shape-shifting alien?
8. What is the first name of the first ever member of the Royal Family to have their tongue pierced?
9. What sort of music would you associate with the Dubliners and the Houghton Weavers?
10. What was the first name of the character in the film *The Sixth Sense* who saw dead people?

QUIZ EIGHT

1. What is the chief constituent of glass?

2. What does the D stand for in the name of the singer kd Lang?

3. Which processed meat product took its name from an abbreviation for spiced ham?

4. In the steak dish Tournedos Rossini what is spread on top of the steak?

5. As what did Siegfried Sassoon achieve fame?

6. What is the name of the large desert situated in China and Mongolia?

7. In the fairytale what is Cinderella's first name?

8. Who became the President of Yugoslavia in 1945?

9. What four-letter word applies to the substance or consistency of wine?

10. What is the world's lowest sea?

QUIZ NINE

1. What is the name of Spain's longest river?
2. What was the real surname of Judy Garland?
3. What was the former name of Thailand?
4. Cnoc Nan Uamh is the name of the deepest what in Scotland?
5. Measuring 6,465 carats the Eminent Star is the world's largest what?
6. In the *Superman* films what was the name of Lex Luthor's sidekick as played by Ned Beatty?
7. The inferior vena cava is the largest what in the human body?
8. What name is given to a water-filled ditch around a castle?
9. What name is given to the end of a magnet?
10. What is mined at the Viburnum Trend mine in Missouri and accounts for just over 10% of the world's output?

QUIZ TEN

1. What is the name of Postman Pat's cat?

2. In which TV series did Neil Morrisey play a character called Rocky?

3. Gareth Blackstock is the lead character in which British sitcom?

4. What is the name of Herman Munster's wife?

5. What was the name of Alf Garnett's daughter as played by Una Stubbs?

6. What was the name of the company founded by Reggie Perrin, after he had left Sunshine Desserts?

7. What four-letter nickname was given to Robbie Coltrane's character in *Cracker*?

8. Who did Dan Blocker play in the 60s western series *Bonanza*?

9. What was the name of the dog in the children's TV programme *The Herbs*?

10. In the same programme what was the name of the owl?

ANSWERS

1. Jess 2. Boon 3. Chef 4. Lily 5. Rita 6. Grot 7. Fitz 8. Hoss 9. Dill 10. Sage

SESSION 6

QUIZ ONE

....

FILL IN THE MISSING FOUR-LETTER WORDS FROM
THE TITLES OF THE FOLLOWING NOVELS
E.G. THE _ _ _ _ WITCH AND THE WARDROBE
BY C S LEWIS (LION)

1. Room With A _ _ _ _ by EM Forster.
2. _ _ _ _ The Obscure by Thomas Hardy.
3. The _ _ _ _ Tycoon by F Scott Fitzgerald.
4. Billy _ _ _ _ by Herman Melville.
5. Eyeless in _ _ _ _ by Aldous Huxley.
6. Hereward the _ _ _ _ by Charles Kingsley.
7. Fanny _ _ _ _ by John Cleland.
8. The _ _ _ _ and Sixpence by Somerset Maugham.
9. _ _ _ _ and Lovers by DH Lawrence.
10. Cancer _ _ _ _ By Alexander Solzhenitsyn.

QUIZ TWO

1. In the Bible what was Lot's wife turned into?
2. In the world of pop music by what four-letter name is Paul Hewson better known?
3. What has an average annual temperature of minus 140 degrees Centigrade?
4. Who composed *The Christmas Oratorio* in the 18th century?
5. What is the surname of the man who is credited with the invention of the cylinder lock?
6. The Caspian Sea is the world's largest what?
7. China is the world's largest producer of which fruit?
8. In the human body the right what has an average weight of 580 grams or 20.5 ounces?
9. Which fizzy drink is advertised on TV as having a totally tropical taste?
10. Which car company was founded in the city of Turin?

QUIZ THREE

1. What is the name of the desert that extends across India and Pakistan and has an approximate area of 259,000 square kilometres (100,000 square miles)?
2. What kind of material is associated with the town of Honiton?
3. Sexton Blake is cockney rhyming slang for a what?
4. What has acquired the nickname of black diamonds?
5. What is Hamley's in London famous for selling?
6. On which record label did Abba record their UK No. 1 hits?
7. After which princess was the Royal Air Force Nursing Service named?
8. Alpha, beta, gamma, delta, epsilon. What comes next?
9. Which four-letter prefix derives from the Greek for below?
10. What is the name of the dog in the *Punch and Judy* shows?

QUIZ FOUR

1. In the Bible what is the name of the home city of Goliath?

2. On which racecourse is the Tote Ebor Handicap run?

3. Under what name did Yasmin Evans have a No. 1 hit?

4. Which supermarket chain was bought out by the American company Walmart?

5. Which former European Cup winners hail from Amsterdam?

6. If equine = horse, what does corvine equal?

7. What is the name of Rab C Nesbitt's son as played on TV by Andrew Fairlie?

8. Which region of Scotland shares its name with a small flute?

9. What is the name of the strait that separates Sri Lanka and India?

10. What is a tope? Is it a frog, a bird or a fish?

ANSWERS
1. Gath 2. York 3. Yazz 4. Asda 5. Ajax 6. Crow 7. Gash 8. Fife 9. Palk 10. Fish –it is a type of shark

QUIZ FIVE

1. Which film was adapted from a novel entitled *Sheep Pig*?
2. In which film did Maurice Chevalier sing 'Thank Heaven For Little Girls'?
3. What is the name of the villain portrayed by Richard Kiel in the Bond films?
4. Which controversial British drama was set in a Borstal and starred Ray Winstone as 'The Daddy'?
5. What was the title of the film in which Julie Andrews played the role of Gertrude Lawrence?
6. What is the name of Inspector Clouseau's oriental valet?
7. What is the first name of Crocodile Dundee?
8. Which sport featured in the film *The Baltimore Bullet*?
9. In which 1985 film did Cher play the mother of a 16-year-old boy who suffered from a disfiguring bone disease?
10. Name the film in which Robin Williams played a character called Peter Banning.

ANSWERS
1. Babe 2. Gigi 3. Jaws 4. Scum 5. Star 6. Kato 7. Mick 8. Pool 9. Mask 10. Hook

QUIZ SIX

1. What was the surname of the famous French fashion designer who died in October 1957?
2. Which river is spanned by the Pulteney Bridge?
3. What name is given to a score of zero for a batsman in cricket?
4. In the *What Katy Did* novels by Susan Coolidge what is the surname of Katy?
5. A papoose is the Native American name for a what?
6. What sort of car does Mr Bean drive?
7. What is the Gaelic name for Ireland?
8. In mythology which part of the body was the weak spot of Achilles?
9. What sort of animal gives its name to a fall in price on the stock exchange?
10. On December 6th 1962 news headlines claimed that what had caused the deaths of 28 London citizens?

ANSWERS
1. Dior 2. Avon 3. Duck 4. Carr 5. Baby 6. Mini 7. Eire 8. Heel 9. Bear 10. Smog

QUIZ SEVEN

1. Des Moines is the capital of which American state?
2. What name is given to the winds that blow over the Adriatic from central Europe?
3. What is the surname of the actress who played the title role in the film *There's Something About Mary*?
4. Egg, larva, butterfly. What stage is missing from the life-cycle of a butterfly?
5. What is the longest river in Northern Ireland?
6. What type of bean with a high protein content is sometimes used as a meat substitute?
7. In the title of the film what was *The African Queen*?
8. What was the name of the rival gang of the Sharks, in the film *West Side Story*?
9. Which female cartoon-strip character was created by Gary Trudeau?
10. What name is given to the traditional dance as performed by Hawaiian women?

ANSWERS
1. Iowa 2. Bora 3. Diaz 4. Pupa 5. Bann 6. Soya 7. Boat 8. Jets 9. Jane 10. Hula

QUIZ EIGHT

1. Which school was founded by Henry IV in 1440?

2. What is the name of Gladys Knight's backing band?

3. What does a cartographer make?

4. Which American group had hit records with 'Drive' and 'Just What I Needed'?

5. If the Hanging Gardens of Babylon were still growing, in which modern-day country would they be found?

6. What is the capital of Qatar?

7. Where in the human body is the carotid artery?

8. What is the name of the straits that separate the north and south islands of New Zealand?

9. What was Julius Caesar told to beware of in the month of March?

10. Which two of the twelve disciples of Jesus had four letters in their name?

QUIZ NINE

1. Bruce Forsythe, Burt Reynolds and Tony Curtis all wear what?
2. What was Old Mother Hubbard hoping to find in her cupboard?
3. Which Danish pop group topped the charts in 1998 with the song 'Dr Jones'?
4. From what type of fruit is the alcoholic beverage slivovitz distilled?
5. What is the first name of Scully in *The X Files*?
6. What first name connects a space hero from the 25th century and the dog in the novel *Call Of The Wild*?
7. Which sports manufacturers took their name from the Greek Goddess of victory?
8. What is the maiden name of Michael Jackson's second wife?
9. Robert Smith is the lead singer with which group who had a Top 10 hit with the song 'The Love Cats'?
10. What name is given to the dance that is by tradition performed at Jewish weddings?

ANSWERS
1.Wigs 2. Bone 3. Aqua 4. Plum 5. Dana 6. Buck 7. Nike 8. Rowe 9.The Cure
10. Hora

QUIZ TEN

1. In which sport is the Cowdray Park Gold Cup contested?
2. Which city hosted the 1952 Winter Olympics?
3. What name is given to the platform from which darts players throw their darts?
4. In which city does Lazio football club play its home matches?
5. What was the name of the horse that won the Epsom Derby in 1999?
6. Name the country that surprisingly won the 1992 Olympic Gold Medal for baseball?
7. What name is given to a feet-first toboggan?
8. Which sport has a name that when translated into English literally means 'The gentle way'?
9. Which was the only football club with four letters in its name to win the FA Cup in the 20th century?
10. The River Effra runs under which famous sporting venue?

ANSWERS
1. Polo 2. Oslo 3. Oche 4. Rome 5. Oath 6. Cuba 7. Luge 8. Judo 9. Bury 10. The Oval

QUIZ ONE

....

NAME THE FILM STARS WITH FOUR-LETTER SURNAMES THAT STARRED IN EACH GROUP OF THREE FILMS.

1. *The Godfather, Eraser* and *Alien Nation.*
2. *The Great Race, The In-Laws* and *The Cheap Detective.*
3. *Mask, Blue Velvet* and *Jurassic Park.*
4. *Magnum Force, Salem's Lot* and *In The Cold Of The Night.*
5. *The Cotton Club, Ferris Bueller's Day Off* and *Dirty Dancing.*
6. *Legends Of The Fall, Thelma and Louise* and *Interview With The Vampire.*
7. *No Mercy, Yanks* and *American Gigolo.*
8. *Peggy Sue Got Married, Twister* and *As Good As It Gets.*
9. *Face Off, Moonstruck* and *Birdy.*
10. *Calamity Jane, The Day Of The Triffids* and *Seven Brides For Seven Brothers.*

ANSWERS

1. James CAAN 2. Peter FALK 3. Laura DERN 4. David SOUL 5. Jennifer GREY 6. Brad PITT 7. Richard GERE 8. Helen HUNT 9. Nicholas CAGE 10. Howard KEEL

66

QUIZ TWO

1. Which hit for the Kinks starts with the line 'I met her in a club down in old Soho'?

2. Which word can mean a fourth of an acre or a cross bearing the image of Christ?

3. From which part of a tree is cinnamon made?

4. What is added to copper to make brass?

5. What is the surname of the first female jockey to compete in the Grand National?

6. What is the surname of the first female jockey to complete the Grand National course?

7. What has been advertised on TV by Henry Cooper, Kevin Keegan & Paul Gascoigne?

8. What is a Sam Browne?

9. What colour is Grumpy the Care Bear?

10. Which pop group topped the UK singles charts in 1971 with a song called 'Hey Girl, Don't Bother Me'?

ANSWERS

1. 'Lola' 2. Rood 3. Bark 4. Zinc 5. Charlotte BREW 6. Geraldine REES 7. Brut 8. A belt 9. Blue 10. The Tams

QUIZ THREE

1. Which part of the body is affected by psoriasis?
2. By what four-letter name did Marie Lawrie become famous?
3. What is the surname of Britain's youngest ever Prime Minister?
4. What sort of meat is used to make mock turtle soup?
5. What is the four-letter ancient name for France?
6. In which month is Father's Day celebrated?
7. *Peter Pan* was originally a song, a play, a book, a poem or a film?
8. According to the Bible who was the first murder victim?
9. What name is given to a male whale?
10. What, originally used as a weapon, was developed into a toy and can perform such manoeuvres as 'Walking the dog' and 'Goes over the mountain'?

ANSWERS
1. Skin 2. Lulu 3. Pitt 4. Veal 5. Gaul 6. June 7. Play 8. Abel 9. Bull 10. Yoyo

QUIZ FOUR

1. Coriander and thyme are both types of what?
2. What kind of oven is used for baking clay pots?
3. What name is given to a small cage for pigeons?
4. What is the backbone of a ship called?
5. What name is given to a shallow point in a river where one can wade across?
6. On a Monopoly board what is sandwiched by Pentonville Road and Pall Mall?
7. Which part of the ear is also the name for part of a leaf?
8. What is the name of the plant with a string-like bark that is used for making ropes?
9. What word describes the colour of a horse which is dark brown mixed with grey?
10. What name is given to the disease affecting corn that blackens the ears of the corn?

QUIZ FIVE

1. Which bird has the best sense of smell?
2. What name is given to the fleshy part of a horse's tail?
3. The great crested is Britain's largest species of what?
4. What name is given to the footprint of a deer?
5. Which is the only breed of dog that has a black tongue?
6. Highland, Welsh Cob and New Forest are all breeds of what?
7. Spider, red and hermit are all types of what?
8. To which bird family does the jay belong?
9. What sort of bird used to be stoned to death to commemorate the execution of St Stephen?
10. What name is given to a male donkey?

QUIZ SIX

1. Their real first names were Leonard, Adolph, Julius, Milton and Herbert. By what four-letter surname were these acting relatives better known?

2. Which alien being did Steve McQueen battle against in his first major film role?

3. What name is given to a mop that is used to clean the deck of a ship?

4. What does a golfer shout as a warning cry?

5. What is the nickname of the second man on the moon?

6. Where in the body is a bone called the patella to be found?

7. What name was given to an Elizabethan frilled collar?

8. Which group had a novelty No. 1 hit with 'Star Trekkin'?

9. What sort of animal was Hartley in the children's TV programme *Pipkins*?

10. Which four-letter word is the title of a film starring the boxer Ken Norton and was also the name of Simon Le Bon's yacht?

ANSWERS

1. The MARX Brothers 2. The Blob 3. Swab 4. 'Fore' 5. Buzz 6. Knee 7. Ruff 8. The Firm 9. Hare 10. *Drum*

QUIZ SEVEN

1. What is the name of the son of Ian Botham who followed in his father's footsteps to become a successful sports star?

2. What name is given to the front of an aeroplane and the front of a skateboard?

3. What name is shared by the inner part of the Earth and the centre of fruit?

4. What name is given to the long pole which is used to suspend a microphone over the actors on a film set?

5. In the fairytale *Beauty and the Beast*, what did Beauty's father steal from the Beast?

6. In which American state was Donny Osmond born?

7. What was the name of the villain in the second *Star Trek* film?

8. By what four-letter acronym is the organisation known that was founded in 1958 to co-ordinate the USA space programme?

9. What type of machine weaves yarn into cloth?

10. By what name was Nickolai Poliakoff known when he was clowning around?

ANSWERS
1. Liam 2. Nose 3. Core 4. Boom 5. A rose 6. Utah 7. Khan 8. NASA 9. Loom 10. Coco

QUIZ EIGHT

1. In 1993 what was the surname of the Vice President of the USA?

2. On the human body, what is the more common name for a naevus?

3. Which disco group had a 1970s smash with 'Le Freak'?

4. In monetary terms what is a pound called in Ireland?

5. Who founded the city of Carthage?

6. What did Denise Royle's surname become when she married Dave in the award-winning sitcom *The Royle Family*?

7. Which two gems are both birthstones for the month of July?

8. By what four-letter name is twilight also known?

9. Which company was founded by Ingvar Kamprach?

10. What connects the nicknames of a Spice Girl and Peterborough FC?

ANSWERS

1. Gore 2. A mole 3. Chic 4. Punt 5. Dido 6. Best 7. Ruby & Onyx 8. Dusk 9. Ikea 10. Posh

QUIZ NINE

1. Which river boasts a tourist attraction known as the Valley of the Kings?
2. What is advertised on TV by Linda Robson and Pauline Quirke?
3. What was the surname of the doctor in EastEnders played by Leonard Fenton?
4. Which lane makes up a set with Mayfair on a Monopoly board?
5. Which actor with a four-letter first name and surname played Batman in the 60s TV series?
6. In *MASH* which part of Major Hoolihan's body were according to her nickname, hot?
7. Charles Lindbergh was which magazine's very first 'Man of the Year'?
8. What is the German word for five?
9. By what name are the string quartet of Haylie, Gay-Yee, Tania and Eos collectively known?
10. What is the first four-letter word to be spoken in the Lord's Prayer?

QUIZ TEN

1. Which Beatles song opens with the line 'When I was younger, so much younger than today'?
2. What is the name of John Lennon's second child?
3. Who with a four-letter first name and surname was the original drummer of the Beatles?
4. What is the first name of John Lennon's second wife?
5. Which four-letter word featured in the title of the Beatles' first UK No. 1 hit single?
6. Which song character was advised to 'Take a sad song and make it better'?
7. Which song character had kaleidoscope eyes?
8. Which Beatles song character was 'Speaking words of wisdom, let it be'?
9. What was the name of the meter maid on the Beatles' *Sergeant Pepper's* album?
10. What is the middle name of Paul McCartney?

ANSWERS

1. 'Help'. 2. Sean 3. Pete Best 4. Yoko 5. From – 'From Me To You'. 6. Jude 7. Lucy 8. Mary 9. Rita 10. Paul – he is called James Paul McCartney

QUIZ ONE

WHAT FOUR-LETTER WORD IS DEFINED AS ...

1. A lasting hostility between two tribes or families?
2. A basin in a harbour where ships are unloaded?
3. A semi-solid lump formed from liquid, especially in the blood?
4. A measure of capacity for dry goods equivalent to two gallons?
5. The left hand side of a ship?
6. The elastic substance in the middle of the sole of a horse's foot?
7. A musical composition for two voices?
8. The characteristic cry of an owl?
9. An aromatic herb with grey/green leaves?
10. A movable stand on which a coffin is placed?

ANSWERS
1. Feud 2. Dock 3. Clot 4. Peck 5. Port 6. Frog 7. Duet 8. Hoot 9. Sage 10. Bier

QUIZ TWO

1. What colour is the largest species of kangaroo?
2. The *Santa Maria*, the *Pinta* and which other ship were used in the historic 1492 voyage of Columbus to America?
3. The philtrum can be found directly below what on the human body?
4. Which bar of chocolate has been advertised on TV by Harry Enfield in company with a number of armadillos?
5. After which saint is the main square in Venice named?
6. In photography what does the L stand for in the initials SLR?
7. If ship = knot, which speed rate does the USS *Enterprise* equate to?
8. Which song title was a hit for Travis in 2001 and the Carpenters in the 1970s?
9. What sort of animals ruled the roost in the novel *Animal Farm*?
10. What name is given to the pungent liquid sprayed by skunks at an aggressor?

ANSWERS

1. Grey 2. *Nina* 3. Nose – it is the name of the groove between the nose and the top lip 4. Dime 5. Mark 6. Lens – Single Lens Reflex 7. Warp 8. 'Sing' 9. Pigs 10. Musk.

QUIZ THREE

....

1. Fill in the missing four-letter word in the following quotation from Benjamin Disraeli: 'There are three types of _ _ _ _, _ _ _ _, damn _ _ _ _ and statistics.'

2. What was the surname of the darts player who achieved the first ever televised nine-dart finish?

3. What was Deirdre's maiden name in *Coronation Street* before she married Ray Langton?

4. What word signifies zero in tennis?

5. What four-letter word beginning with T is the name given to a small lake surrounded by mountains?

6. Five and a half yards make up one what?

7. What name is given to the ruler of an emirate?

8. Which Latin phrase consisting of two four-letter words literally means 'In good faith'?

9. What is the name of the holy hill in Jerusalem?

10. How is Elvis Presley's middle name spelt on his gravestone?

ANSWERS

1. Lies 2. Lowe 3. Hunt 4. Love 5. Tarn 6. Pole 7. Emir 8. Bona fide 9. Zion 10. Aron – it should be spelt 'Aaron' which fuelled speculation that he was still alive

78

QUIZ FOUR

1. What is made up of protons and neutrons in a central nucleus surrounded by electrons?
2. TG is the international car registration plate for where?
3. Which king ruled the house of Plantagenet from 1199 to 1216?
4. Which grammatical part of a sentence names a person, an animal or an object?
5. The larkspur and the water-lily are the birth flowers of which month?
6. Who is the Roman goddess of the moon?
7. Which liquid measure is equal to a quarter of a pint in the USA, and five fluid ounces in the UK?
8. What four-letter word is police jargon for fingerprints?
9. Which Italian word is used as a greeting or a farewell?
10. What name was given to the type of jacket worn by members of the military that had metal plates sewn into the lining as protection against bullets?

ANSWERS
1. An atom 2. Togo 3. John 4. Noun 5. July 6. Luna 7. Gill 8. Dabs 9. Ciao – pronounced chow 10. Flak

QUIZ FIVE

....

NAME THE POP GROUPS WITH FOUR LETTERS IN THEIR NAME FROM EACH PAIR OF HIT RECORDS.

1. 'Need You Tonight' and 'Mystify'.
2. 'Common People' and 'Disco 2000'.
3. 'Knock Three Times' and 'Tie A Yellow Ribbon Round The Old Oak Tree'.
4. 'Country House' and 'Beetlebum'.
5. 'Wishing Well' and 'All Right Now'.
6. 'Telegram Sam' and 'Metal Guru'.
7. 'Sandstorm' and 'Guiding Star'.
8. 'Africa' and 'Hold The Line'.
9. 'Alone Without You' and 'Love and Pride'.
10. 'Come Back Brighter' and 'Place Your Hands'.

QUIZ SIX

1. What title is taken by a Hindu spiritual teacher?
2. Which slang word for food is also the name given to the worm-like larva of certain insects?
3. Which colour of a yellowish/brown is also the name of a young deer?
4. What name is given to a star that suddenly erupts and magnifies its brightness?
5. What is the singular of ova?
6. The name of which ancient Peruvian civilisation literally translates into English as 'King'?
7. Which age followed the Bronze Age?
8. What was the four-letter nickname of sports star George Herman Ruth?
9. What name was given to the Russian parliament established in 1905 in the wake of the Revolution?
10. Which basic structural unit of life is the smallest unit capable of independent existence?

ANSWERS
1. Guru 2. Grub 3. Fawn 4. Nova 5. Ovum 6. Inca 7. Iron 8. Babe 9. Duma 10. A cell

QUIZ SEVEN

1. What is the real first name of the rap star Puff Daddy?

2. What is the name of the strip, a disputed area of land that lies between Israel and Egypt?

3. In which country does a sultanate rule in the capital city of Muscat?

4. What type of music was named in Chicago and has the main characteristic of a syncopated rhythmic beat, with improvisation of a musical theme?

5. Which two-word phrase, both words containing four letters, means 'trusty scout' and was often uttered by Tonto?

6. In music, LP signified which two four-letter words?

7. What name for an inflatable brand of airbed was originally registered as a trade name by PB Cow and Company?

8. Margaretha Zelle, the Dutch spy during World War I, adopted which pseudonym that consisted of two four-letter names?

9. Which fruit provided the nickname of the author PG Wodehouse?

10. Name the five American presidents, up to and including the year 2001, that had four-letter surnames.

ANSWERS

1. Sean 2. Gaza 3. Oman 4. Jazz 5. Kemo sabe 6. Long play 7. Lilo 8. Mata Hari 9. Plum 10. Bush (Jnr and Snr), Ford, Taft and Polk

QUIZ EIGHT

1. What name is given to a group of leopards?

2. What is the surname of the American business-man who died in May 2001 aged 74, and became famous after appearing in a TV advert for Remington shavers in which he said 'I liked the shaver so much I bought the company'?

3. Which word is missing from the following proverb? 'Faint heart never won fair _ _ _ _'

4. Who did Mehmet Ali Agca attempt to assassinate in 1981?

5. By what name is Dave Evans of pop group U2 also known?

6. Which two types of patterns of fingerprints have four-letter names?

7. What is the name of the sacred river in the poem 'Kubla Khan' by Samuel Taylor Coleridge?

8. What is the name of the DIY expert in the TV programme *Changing Rooms*?

9. Candlestick, revolver, lead piping, knife and spanner. Which murder weapon is missing from the board game of Cluedo?

10. Which is the only room with a four-letter name in the board game of Cluedo?

QUIZ NINE

1. What is the national airline of Jordan?
2. What was the name of the Kray twins' underworld gang in the 1960s?
3. Which four-letter acronym is the South African Secret Service known by?
4. Which Russian title was taken by Peter the Great and Nicholas II?
5. If Chicago = bears and Miami = dolphins, what does Los Angeles =?
6. Where do Southampton FC play their home matches?
7. Which prefix means one thousand millionth?
8. What does a chronometer measure?
9. What was the name of the Flintstones' family pet?
10. Which fashion label was founded by Barbara Hulanicki?

ANSWERS

1.Alia 2.The Firm 3. BOSS – Bureau of State Security 4.Tsar 5. Rams 6.The Dell 7. Nano 8.Time 9. Dino 10. Biba

QUIZ TEN

WHAT IS STUDIED BY THE FOLLOWING 'OLOGISTS' OR FEARED IN THE FOLLOWING PHOBIAS?

1. Algophobia
2. Pedologist
3. Mysophobia
4. Ichthyologist
5. Pyrophobia
6. Rhinologist
7. Apiphobia
8. Oologist
9. Ergophobia
10. Nyctophobia

ANSWERS
1. Pain 2. Soil 3. Dirt 4. Fish 5. Fire 6. The nose 7. Bees 8. Eggs 9. Work 10. The dark

SESSION 9

QUIZ ONE

WHAT FOUR-LETTER WORD IS DEFINED AS ...

1. A statue depicting the head and shoulders of a person?
2. To burn until black?
3. A wooden frame joining oxen?
4. Part of a canal for raising or lowering boats?
5. A chain of rocks lying near the surface of the sea?
6. A sailing vessel with two masts and square cut sails?
7. A passage for air and smoke in a stove or chimney?
8. One hundredth of a dollar?
9. A night of watching by the side of a dead body?
10. A thin-soled shoe or an instrument for raising water?

QUIZ TWO

THE ANSWERS TO THE FOLLOWING QUESTIONS ALL REQUIRE THE NAME OF A WOMAN WITH A FOUR-LETTER FIRST NAME AND SURNAME.

1. Which singer was backed by the Blackhearts on the song 'I Love Rock And Roll'?

2. Who played Mo Butcher in *EastEnders*?

3. Who married American President Abraham Lincoln?

4. Which fictional character has been played on film by Margot Kidder and on TV by Teri Hatcher?

5. In 1997 who had a hit record with a song called 'Professional Widow'?

6. Which founder member of TV-AM was also ITV's first female national newsreader?

7. Who released the albums *The Kick Inside* and *Lionheart*?

8. Who plays Nellie Boswell in *Bread*?

9. Who am I? I was born in May 1930 and I have appeared in *Only Fools and Horses* and *Just William* on TV. I will be best remembered as a *Carry On* actress and in the film *Carry On Henry*, I played one of the wives of Henry VIII.

10. Name the folk-singer who had her biggest hit in 1971 with the song 'The Night They Drove Old Dixie Down'.

ANSWERS

1. Joan Jett 2. Edna Dore 3. Mary Todd 4. Lois Lane 5. Tori Amos 6. Anna Ford 7. Kate Bush 8. Jean Boht 9. Joan Sims 10. Joan Baez

QUIZ THREE

THE ANSWERS TO THE FOLLOWING QUESTIONS ALL REQUIRE THE NAME OF A MAN WITH A FOUR-LETTER FIRST NAME AND SURNAME.

1. Which former husband of Madonna was jailed for assault?

2. Who committed suicide shortly after the death of his wife Diana Dors?

3. Who played a character called Henry Willows in the sitcom *Home To Roost*?

4. Who created Wallace and Grommit?

5. Who killed Lee Harvey Oswald?

6. Who on TV has appeared in adverts for Gold Blend and the TV series *Buffy The Vampire Slayer*?

7. Who played Hawkeye in the TV version of *MASH*?

8. Who was the British government's defence secretary between 1981 and 1983?

9. Who said 'Religion is the opium of the people'?

10. Who wrote the novels *Exodus* and *Armageddon*?

ANSWERS

1. Sean Penn 2. Alan Lake 3. John Thaw 4. Nick Park 5. Jack Ruby 6. Tony Head 7. Alan Alda 8. John Nott 9. Karl Marx 10. Leon Uris

QUIZ FOUR

FILL IN THE MISSING FOUR-LETTER WORDS FROM THE LIST OF NO. I HITS.

E.G. 1983 – '_ _ _ _ Under' by Men At Work. = Down

1. 1969 – '_ _ _ _ the _ _ _ _' by the Scaffold.
2. 1996 – 'Return of the _ _ _ _' by Mark Morrison.
3. 1985 – '_ _ _ _Lover' by Philip Bailey and Phil Collins.
4. 1972 – 'You _ _ _ _ It _ _ _ _' by Rod Stewart.
5. 1998 – 'Bootie _ _ _ _' by All Saints.
6. 1970 – '_ _ _ _ Of _ _ _ _' by Freda Payne.
7. 1964 – '_ _ _ _ All _ _ _ _' by the Dave Clark Five.
8. 1963 – 'Wayward _ _ _ _' by Frank Ifield.
9. 1996 – 'A Different _ _ _ _' by Boyzone.
10. 1956 – '16 _ _ _ _' by Tennessee Ernie Ford.

QUIZ FIVE

1. What is the French word for green?
2. Which three Latin four-letter words translate into English as 'I came, I saw, I conquered'?
3. Which Dutch town gave its name to a famous mild round cheese?
4. What name is given to a Muslim's pilgrimage to Mecca?
5. What is yeasted bread in an Indian restaurant called?
6. What is the German word for 'No'?
7. Who is the patron saint of Norway?
8. What is the name of the ceremonial dance performed by the All Blacks Rugby Union team?
9. Which Latin word means 'I forbid' in English?
10. Which word from the Hindu language translates into English as 'union'?

ANSWERS
1.Vert 2.Veni, vidi, vici 3.Edam 4.Hajj 5.Naan 6.Nein 7.Olaf 8.Haka 9.Veto 10.Yoga

QUIZ SIX

WHICH FOUR-LETTER WORD CAN MEAN . . .

1. A sharp pull or a slang name for an American?
2. To stumble or a journey?
3. A nobleman ranked below a prince or John Wayne's nickname?
4. A type of tree or to long for?
5. A third of a yard or part of the body?
6. The hide of an animal or to throw things at?
7. A small dagger or a boy's first name?
8. A swollen sore or to heat water?
9. A ticket allowing one to go somewhere or a gap between mountains?
10. Part of a harbour or the plant family to which rhubarb belongs?

ANSWERS
1.Yank 2.Trip 3. Duke 4.Pine 5. Foot 6. Pelt 7. Dirk 8. Boil 9. Pass 10. Dock

QUIZ SEVEN

BACK TO FRONT FOUR-LETTER WORDS
E.G. FORWARDS IT IS A GREEK GOD AND BACKWARDS IT IS A CANAL. ANSWER = ZEUS AND SUEZ

1. Forwards it is part of a hospital and backwards it means to make a picture.

2. Forwards it means to puncture with a knife and backwards it is the only mammals capable of true flight.

3. Forwards it is the name of a sport and backwards it means to whip.

4. Forwards it is part of a fishing rod and backwards it means to stare at lustfully.

5. Forwards it means to eat and backwards it is the first name of the creator of Noddy.

6. Forwards it is the Greek god of love and backwards it can mean a wound or a cut.

7. Forwards it means to pack tightly together and backwards it is the first name of the lead singer of Soft Cell.

8. Forwards it is the animal from which buckskin is obtained and backwards it is the name of a long grass found in marshland.

9. Forwards they are types of firearm and backwards it means comfortable.

10. Forwards it is the name of a TV gladiator and backwards it means the movement of a river.

ANSWERS
1. Ward and Draw 2. Stab and Bats 3. Golf and Flog 4. Reel and Leer 5. Dine and Enid 6. Eros and Sore 7. Cram and Marc 8. Deer and Reed 9. Guns and Snug 10. Wolf and Flow

QUIZ EIGHT

WHAT IS THE FIRST NAME OF THE CHARACTER PLAYED BY ...

1. David McCallum in *The Man From UNCLE*?
2. Frances de la Tour in *Rising Damp*?
3. John Thaw in *The Sweeney*?
4. David Schwimmer in *Friends*?
5. George Wendt in *Cheers*?

WHAT IS THE SURNAME OF THE CHARACTER PLAYED BY ...

6. Priscilla Presley in *Dallas*?
7. William Shatner in *Star Trek*?
8. Katherine Helmond in *Soap*?
9. Ian Lavender in *Dad's Army*?
10. Amanda Donohoe in *LA Law*?

ANSWERS

1. Ilya 2. Ruth 3. Jack 4. Ross 5. Norm 6. Wade 7. Kirk 8. Tate 9. Pike 10. Lamb

QUIZ NINE

WHAT IS THE FIRST NAME OF THE CHARACTER PLAYED BY . . .

1. Julie Christie in *Dr Zhivago*?
2. Humphrey Bogart in *Casablanca*?
3. Kevin Kline in *A Fish Called Wanda*?
4. Robert De Niro in *Raging Bull*?
5. Mark Hamill in *Star Wars*?

WHAT IS THE SURNAME OF THE CHARACTER PLAYED BY . . .

6. Harrison Ford in *Star Wars*?
7. Gary Cooper in *High Noon*?
8. Orson Wells in *The Third Man*?
9. Grace Kelly in *High Society*?
10. John Travolta in *Grease*?

QUIZ TEN

1. What did the ugly duckling turn into?
2. Which novel by Stephen King told the story of a rabid St Bernard dog?
3. Which novel by Frank Herbert was adapted into a film starring Sting?
4. What is the name of the pet raven in the Dickens novel *Barnaby Rudge?*
5. What was the home city of *Robinson Crusoe?*
6. What is the name of the villain in Shakespeare's *Othello?*
7. Which two members of the Famous Five have four-letter first names?
8. What is the name of the captain of the *Nautilus* in the Jules Verne novel *20,000 Leagues Under The Sea?*
9. In the Dickens novel *Dombey & Son*, what is the first name of the son?
10. What is the last word in the Bible?

ANSWERS
1. A swan 2. *Cujo* 3. *Dune* 4. Grip 5. York 6. Iago 7. Anne and Dick 8. Nemo 9. Paul 10. Amen